Animals with Strength
Gorillas

by Julie Murray

Dash!
LEVELED READERS
An Imprint of Abdo Zoom • abdobooks.com

Level 1 – Beginning
Short and simple sentences with familiar words or patterns for children who are beginning to understand how letters and sounds go together.

Level 2 – Emerging
Longer words and sentences with more complex language patterns for readers who are practicing common words and letter sounds.

Level 3 – Transitional
More developed language and vocabulary for readers who are becoming more independent.

THIS BOOK CONTAINS RECYCLED MATERIALS

abdobooks.com

Published by Abdo Zoom, a division of ABDO, PO Box 398166, Minneapolis, Minnesota 55439. Copyright © 2023 by Abdo Consulting Group, Inc. International copyrights reserved in all countries. No part of this book may be reproduced in any form without written permission from the publisher. Dash!™ is a trademark and logo of Abdo Zoom.

Printed in the United States of America, North Mankato, Minnesota.
102022
012023

Photo Credits: Alamy, Getty Images, Minden Pictures, Shutterstock
Production Contributors: Kenny Abdo, Jennie Forsberg, Grace Hansen, John Hansen
Design Contributors: Candice Keimig, Neil Klinepier

Library of Congress Control Number: 2022937226

Publisher's Cataloging in Publication Data

Names: Murray, Julie, author.
Title: Gorillas / by Julie Murray
Description: Minneapolis, Minnesota : Abdo Zoom, 2023 | Series: Animals with strength | Includes online resources and index.
Identifiers: ISBN 9781098280031 (lib. bdg.) | ISBN 9781098280567 (ebook) | ISBN 9781098280864 (Read-to-Me ebook)
Subjects: LCSH: Gorilla--Juvenile literature. | Gorilla--Behavior--Juvenile literature. | Muscle strength--Juvenile literature. | Primates--Juvenile literature. | Zoology--Juvenile literature.
Classification: DDC 599.884--dc23

Table of Contents

Gorillas 4

More Facts 22

Glossary 23

Index 24

Online Resources 24

Gorillas

Gorillas are found in Africa. They live in forests.

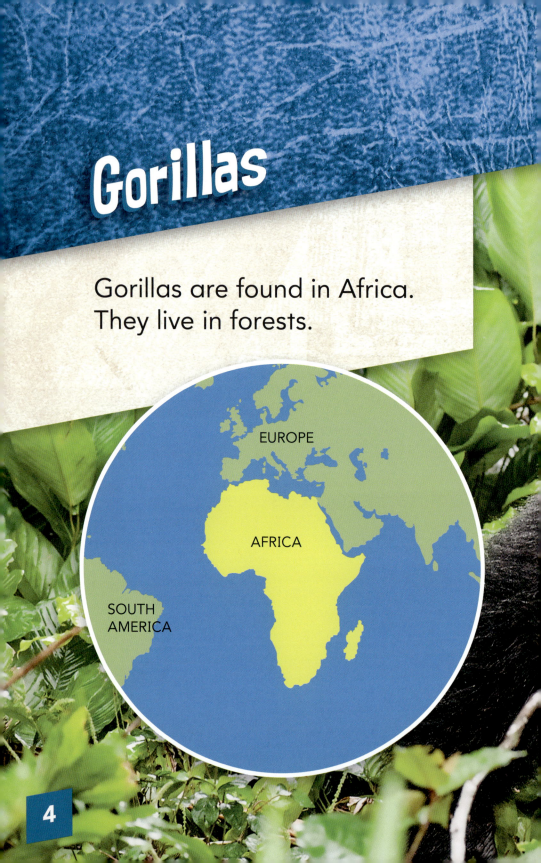

They are big animals! Males can be six feet (1.8 m) tall. They can weigh 400 pounds (181 kg).

Gorillas have dark hair that covers most of their body.

Gorillas have long arms. Their legs are shorter. They walk on all four **limbs**.

Gorilla hands are like human hands. They can grab and hold items.

Gorillas mainly eat plants and fruit. They can eat 50 pounds (23 kg) of food each day!

They are **social** animals. They spend time **grooming** each other.

Gorillas are strong! **Silverbacks** are the largest and strongest.

A **silverback** is 20 times stronger than a human. It can lift 4,000 pounds (1,810 kg)!

More Facts

- Gorillas live in groups called bands or troops.

- They can run up to 25 miles per hour (40 kph).

- They are smart! They can even learn sign language.

Glossary

groom – to care for and make clean.

limb – a part of the body that can move and bend. Arms, legs, and wings are limbs.

silverback – a mature male gorilla distinguished by a silvery white or gray area across its back.

social – living in groups and communities instead of alone.

Index

Africa 4
food 14
habitat 4
habits 17
hair 9
hands 12

limbs 11
males 6
silverback 18, 21
size 6
strength 18, 21
weight 6

Online Resources

To learn more about gorillas, please visit **abdobooklinks.com** or scan this QR code. These links are routinely monitored and updated to provide the most current information available.